Phased

A.B. MASTERS

CONTENTS

READ THIS FIRST

When I was in law school, my husband and I spent a summer working on a research project in Uganda. This afforded us opportunities to go on safaris and to hike deep into Uganda's jungles and forests. All of the national parks that we visited required us to hike and explore with a Ugandan guide.

At first, this bothered us; after all, part of what we love most about being in nature is the privacy and peace of being alone. But, we had been warned about some of the dangers of hiking alone, particularly in one national forest that bordered the Congo. Purportedly, rebels from the Congo had kidnapped foreigners in recent months. In addition, there were mountain gorillas, leopards, lions, and a host of other wild animals that we were simply not trained to encounter. Many of the trails were unmarked. The guides knew how to track the animals, had a good sense of where the animals would be in the jungle, and were equipped with the necessary skills and tools in the event of an attack. They knew the trails. They knew the jungle. We did not. It was clear that there was safety in using a guide.

Just like there was safety in navigating Ugandan jungles with a guide, there is safety in navigating your physical fitness and financial matters with a guide. In truth, you could attempt either of these practices on your own. And the odds are, you have probably tried. The tools that this program will give you will allow you to successfully and smartly navigate your physical and financial fitness.

Roughly sixty percent of Americans have less than $500 in savings. And roughly thirty-four percent have no savings at all.[i] In addition, one in three Americans are considered overweight.[ii] Why, in the land of the free, where our financial opportunities are practically limitless, do we struggle so much with our finances? Why, in a nation where we have good, clean, healthy food, do we struggle so much with our physical fitness? In other developed nations, the statistics are not quite so stark, but the trend is the same in that individuals in wealthy nations are not putting money towards savings and also have rising obesity and weight related health issues. Why?

In this book, we will explore the underlying problems we face in working out our finances and physical fitness to help us conquer both. But before we get there, I am going to let you in on a little secret. It is something that many people in the fitness or financial industries would not want me to share with you. Are you ready?

Here it is.

Almost any physical fitness program out there will work for you. Almost any financial program out there will work for you. Indeed, you can succeed on almost any kind of program out there. Think about that.

There are hundreds of different strategies and programs out there that you could use to get your physical fitness on track. There are plenty of personal finance programs out there. So what makes the difference on whether or not you succeed? The extent to which you engage in the program.

Perhaps you have heard the adage "you reap what you sow." Well it's true. That which you put into something is typically that what you get out. This applies to fitness programs, marriages, friendships, work, and a host of other situations. And it certainly applies to *Phased*. The extent to which you engage in this program is the extent to which you will succeed in this program.

Have you ever started a diet and eventually given up? Have you ever set a budget and eventually started overspending again? Take a moment to think about why you did not succeed. Was it too complicated? Was there some product you simply could not pass up—even though you were already over budget?

You can improve your finances and physical fitness.

This program was designed specifically for YOU—to simplify both your finances and your physical fitness. Because you know what? When things are too complicated or involved, they often don't stick. Most of us are too busy for complicated. The fact of the matter is that life is often needlessly complicated. When things are too complicated, it makes it difficult to stay engaged. Fitness and finances should be simple. I don't mean to say that this program will be easy—it won't. While this program has simplified your physical and financial fitness and will equip you with the tools that you need to succeed in both aspects, in the end, your success in this program will depend on you. You are going to have to challenge yourself to stay on track. You are going to have to engage. At some point, you might find yourself off track and you will have to pull it together and get back on track. But you will have a simple program that will target your goals head on and will help you every step of the way. **You have to be willing to fight for yourself** and your family to get your physical fitness and finances on track.

Are you ready?

HOW TO USE THIS BOOK

I recommend the following strategy to read this book. First, skim over it—read the entire book somewhat quickly to get a general overview for what you will be doing for the next ten weeks. Then, jump in and start the program. Each section of this book is divided into different Phases of the program. Each Phase hones in on a principle that must become a part of who you are in order to achieve long-term physical and financial fitness. A table of contents has been provided for you at the beginning of the book to make it easy to thumb to whatever Phase you are working on. Highlight parts that stand out to you. Refer back to these pages often. If you write your goals in this book, be sure to come back and review them frequently.

The program starts with Phase I. You will stay on that Phase until you have completed each task associated with the Phase. Then you will move on and start reading and working on the next Phase and continue on until you have completed all five Phases.

After you have completed all of the Phases, and the accompanying workouts, you will have officially "Phased" and will be well on your way to achieving all of the financial and physical fitness goals that you have for yourself. The Phases combine to form the cheesy but memorable acronym, PHASE.

Phase I: Make **P**lans
Phase II: The Art of **H**opefulness
Phase III: **A**bility
Phase IV: **S**elf-Control
Phase V: **E**valuation

THINGS TO KNOW BEFORE YOU START

I. MONEY MEETINGS

Every week you will have a money meeting to assess your finances. If you have a spouse or significant other (or anyone with whom you share money), you will take time once a week to sit with them to have a money meeting. You should continue this practice throughout your life—even after you have completed this program.

The purpose of the money meeting is to assess your finances and make sure you are staying on track. Each week at the meeting, you will track your spending for the prior week—accounting for each dollar that you spent. If you bank online, review your spending using your bank account. If you use cash, be sure to save receipts so you can note where each dollar went over the week. In addition, you will discuss unanticipated expenditures. You will create savings accounts. You will plan where each dollar goes.

You will also analyze your financial goals—creating, refining, and refocusing on them. You will, later in this program, create a budget at a money meeting. Then, at future money meetings, you will work to refine this budget until it works well for you. You should think about and discuss upcoming expenses that you may need to save for. Reevaluate your financial goals as needed.

How will you accomplish all of this? First, schedule a regular time once per week to have a money meeting. My spouse and I hold our money meetings every Sunday evening. This is a good time for us because it allows us to start out the week focused on our goals. It is also a day where we are more likely to be home and undistracted from the other activities of the week. It is a convenient time for us and that is precisely the point—you will need to pick a time that works for you and that will continue to work for you.

You should consider your money meeting one of the most important items on your to do list each week. *Never* miss a money meeting. It can be rescheduled to accommodate your needs but it should never be forgotten. Money meetings are essential to your financial success. It is the time that you will dedicate to learning about your money—where it is going and where you want it to go. You cannot achieve personal finance success without being intimately involved with your money. Ask yourself hard questions at this meeting, like, how was your spending this week? Did you eat out too much? Did you spend less than anticipated? How can you improve? Did you have an unexpected expense arise, such as car maintenance?

At your first money meeting, discuss your financial goals. Write down each goal and if you share money with someone else, review your goals together. Come up with financial goals that you can work towards together (more on this in Phase I). Talk about the changes you will make to help one another achieve your goals and how to achieve your goals together.

II. YOUR NUTRITION

There are three cylinders that need to be firing together in order to efficiently achieve almost any fitness goal: (1) nutrition, (2) cardio, and (3) strength training. You can eat terribly and still lose weight working out. You could also lose weight doing cardio and no strength training. You could add muscle and burn fat by strength training without paying much attention to cardio and nutrition. But to do it most effectively, you must be firing from all three cylinders.

Your goal in eating should be to fuel your body with the nutrients that it needs to thrive and power you through not only your workouts, but your whole day. You will eat a variety of complex carbohydrates, proteins, fruits, and vegetables. You will pair protein with meals to facilitate muscle growth and satiety, as follows:

Protein pairing:

Throughout this program, you will eat 6 meals a day. Not more, not less. Each meal will pair protein with carbs (protein pairing) and frequently, a vegetable. For the purposes of this program, consider fruit as a carb. You may add small amounts of fat to any meal. The size of your meals should be about the size of your fist as a general rule of thumb. You should eat so that you are satiated, but not overly full.

For example, you could combine grilled chicken with sweet potatoes and broccoli as a meal. Or perhaps fat-free Greek yogurt with strawberries. You may add small amounts of fat to any meal. The last meal of the day should not include a carbohydrate. There are sound reasons why you should eat carbohydrates throughout the day—they provide the energy you will need to work out hard. They provide glucose which proffers brain power. Many whole grains contain important B vitamins which help convert energy from food and help your body make red blood cells. Eat carbohydrates for energy. When you are preparing to go to bed at night, you do not need that extra energy.

Note the following lists of *Phased* approved foods with an accompanying example of what a day of eating might look like for you on the following page:

Phased approved carbs:

Brown rice
Wild rice
Sweet potatoes
Whole/steel cut oats
Fruit
Carrots
Quinoa
Corn
Whole wheat
Whole grains

Phased approved protein:

Eggs
Chicken
Lean turkey
Lean cuts of red meat (90% or greater),
Fat-free low-sugar dairy products such as Greek
yogurt
Protein supplements such as protein bars and
protein drinks, especially directly after a work out
Note that this is not a complete list. The idea is
simply that you should choose lean proteins.

Phased approved vegetables:

Any vegetables that rank low on the glycemic index and have low fat are fair game in this program. Some especially good options noted for their high protein and low calorie count include:

Broccoli
Peas
Spinach
Kale
Onion
Brussel Sprouts
Asparagus
Cabbage
Bell Peppers
Zucchini
Green Beans

Special note: carrots and corn rank higher on the glycemic index than most vegetables, so they should be considered a carb in this program and should be used moderately.

Phased Fats:

Fats should be used in moderation. You may add one serving of fat to no more than 3 meals per day.

Avocado or avocado oil (1 serving = ¼ an avocado)
Natural cheese (read: not American cheese) (1 serving = ¼ cup of shredded cheese)
Olive oil (1 serving =1 tsp)
Coconut oil (1 serving =1 tsp)

Watch out for: high glycemic fruits and vegetables and overeating high calorie foods like avocado and cheese. What is the glycemic index? It is an index that measures how quickly carbohydrates in food cause blood sugar levels to rise after eating and how quickly those carbs convert to glucose.

So what's the beef with high glycemic foods? There is nothing necessarily "wrong" with foods that rate high on the glycemic index. Many of these fruits and vegetables have nutritious value. It just means that those foods usually cause a rapid spike in blood sugar levels. As your body tries to regulate itself after a surge in blood sugar and insulin, it sends messages to your brain that you need more sugar, creating a desire in you to eat more of that (or other) food. You can see for weight loss purposes how this could cause trouble—it becomes harder to resist over eating. You don't have to avoid these foods—just be aware of them, and don't over eat them. Always pair them with proteins to induce satiety.

> *Examples of high glycemic fruits:* grapes, watermelon, cherries, bananas

> *Examples of high glycemic vegetables:* corn, carrots (considered carbs in this program),

Remember: No meals after 8:00 p.m. (let your body digest) UNLESS you are working out after 8:00 p.m. Eat to refuel your muscles with only protein after the workout. Also note that the last meal of the day should not include a carb.

Here is an example day of what you could eat in a day:
Breakfast: Greek yogurt with fresh strawberries
Snack: egg, cheese, whole grain bagel
Lunch: chicken, brown rice, salad
Snack: string cheese, apple
Dinner: Tilapia, brown rice, green beans
Snack: Protein drink

SUMMARY OF NUTRITION PLAN:

1. Eat 6 meals each day, 1 meal every 2-3 hours
2. In every meal, pair a carb (like brown rice) with a protein (like chicken) with the exception of the last meal of the day (protein and vegetables only).
3. Add small amounts fat (like ¼ of an avocado) to any meal you would like.
4. Eat only "good" carbs (see Phased approved carb list)
5. Take it easy on foods that rate high on the glycemic index.

III. YOUR FITNESS

What would happen if, for no good reason, you simply did not show up for work one day? Would you be reprimanded? Fired? Would it damage your reputation at work?

Many of us, for no good reason, fail to work out. When in reality, working out should be as important as showing up for work every day. After all, its effects are far-reaching. Working out improves your quality of life both immediately and over the course of your life. Taking a little bit of time each day to invest in yourself will make you a better person. Exercise has been shown to make employees more productive at work.[iii] It boosts self-esteem. It makes it easier to make healthy food choices. It aids in self-control. Accordingly, it influences almost all aspects of any relationship you have. Never feel guilty about taking time to work out. It will help you be a better spouse, parent, friend, employer, employee, or any other role you play in your life. Thirty to sixty minutes a day goes a long way.

A note about the fitness portion of this program—you do not have to follow these workouts if you do not wish to do so. You may choose ANY program that will give you four to six workouts per week for ten weeks. For example, in Phase I, you will set fitness goals. Altering the workouts might be a good idea for people who have fitness goals of doing something like running a marathon—your workouts would simply be substituted with whatever training you need to get yourself ready for the marathon. If you prefer to lift heavy weights in a gym and your budget affords you a gym pass, please feel free to follow any weightlifting program. There are a number of free options you can access online. The only rule is that you must workout in some form of another four to six times per week plus one day of active rest. Active rest includes things like going for a casual swim or walk.

That being said, these workouts have been prepared with you in mind—all can be done from the comfort of your home or modified to do in a gym. They require very little equipment. If you follow these workouts exactly and stick to your nutrition guide, you will get into excellent shape. If you choose to do these from home, you may want to invest in exercise bands that come with handles. Many can be found online for less than $20.

WORKOUT EXPLANATIONS:

FOR SPEED = as fast as you can

5x50 =5 sets of 50

SUPERSET = perform the exercises together. For example, if the work out says 2x30 jumping lunges and the next says 2x20 lying leg curls (like in the first workout) you would do 1 set of 30 jumping lunges and then 1 set of 20 leg curls. Then, repeat. That's a superset.

CARDIO: Unless the workout indicates otherwise, anytime the workout lists "cardio," you can do any form of cardio you wish. You can swim, walk, run, hike, dance, jump rope, or do anything else that gets your heart pumping for the allotted amount of time. Cardio sessions can be done at a separate time than the strength training sessions. The first cardio of the day should ideally be done before your first meal of the day, as indicated by "fasted" on the cardio.

If you don't understand any other terminology in the workouts, you can do a quick internet search to find the meaning. For example, if you don't know what a "bow pose" looks like, do a quick internet search and you will find images and video tutorials if you need them. I've tried to make the workouts easily readable so that while you are working out, you don't have to stop and look things up. But before you work out, quickly read through the workout and look up anything you don't understand.

IV. PLANNING AND PREPARING MEALS

Each week, you will take time to plan and prepare meals for the upcoming week. Planning meals ahead of time makes you more likely to choose healthy foods. In fact, according to the American Journal of Preventive Medicine, meal planning is associated with a greater intake of fruits, vegetables, and lean proteins.[iv] People who meal prep also spend less money on food generally, including less money on eating out.[v] Want to be successful with your fitness and financial goals? Start meal prepping.

Get Started.

Start by looking up your local grocer's ad for foods that are on sale. Make a list of meals that you enjoy that could incorporate those food items that are on sale. Incorporate foods that are within the nutrition guidelines. Note that most stores repeat sales every five to eight weeks. If there is a food item that you know you and your family will eat, stock up for five to eight weeks on that item so you know you are getting the best price on the item (saving even more money).

For even more savings, pair those on-sale items with coupons or rebates. You can find coupons online, in your newspaper, and using cash back apps on a smart phone.

Spend a couple of hours over the weekend preparing your meals. Divide them into personal sized portions and store them in the freezer. That way, when it is time for you to eat, you will reach for a prepped meal instead of racing to the drive-thru at your favorite fast food restaurant. You can also freeze meals in family-sized portions so that you have quick dinners on hand for a family meal.

Remember, the extent to which you are prepared is the extent to which you will succeed. Take the time to plan and prepare your meals and your grocery list accordingly. A small amount of time dedicated to preparation and planning will set you on track all week long.

PHASE I

MAKE PLANS

"A goal without a **plan** is just a wish."
— Antoine de Saint-Exupéry

The first step toward achieving financial and physical fitness is to create well-thought out plans for both your financial and physical fitness. Creating good plans is essential to your success in this program.

Imagine you are given a large sum of money to build your dream home. It is the perfect amount of money to build the perfect home with every detail you desire. What would this home look like? Is there a resort style pool? A golf course out back? An oversized master bedroom with a walk-in closet that goes on for days? Take a moment to think about what your dream home would look like. Imagine all of its unique features. Open the front door and walk into your home in your mind. What do you see? Is there a grand entryway? Are there large windows that give you a view out back? What is your view? Are you on the beach? Overlooking a big city?

How would you begin construction of this home? Would you start pouring a foundation and nailing pieces together, and just kind of hope for a good outcome? Or perhaps would create a well-thought plan, seeking the guidance of an architect, engineers, and other professionals to help you conjure up a plan to build your dream home?

Of course you would have a plan! Building a dream home without a plan seems absurd, doesn't it? A dream home should be perfect. It should be everything you have ever wanted out of a home.

Consider your physical and financial fitness as you would your dream house. Begin to build them just as you would your dream home—with a well-thought-out plan. After all, your physical and financial fitness should be everything you want them to be. And they can. But it all starts with forming plans—and then following through.

In Phase I, the first two weeks of this program, you will be focusing on creating plans for your physical and financial fitness. In the book *No Excuses* by Brian Tracy, he offers, "the very act of thinking and planning unlocks your mental powers, triggers your creativity, and increases your mental and physical energies."[vi] Indeed, you can accomplish much more with a plan than you ever could without one. The mere act of creating a plan focuses your energy and allows you to conjure up ideas that otherwise may never have occurred to you to help you achieve your goals.

With a well-thought plan, you will find it easier not only to get going, but to *keep* going when times get tough. Your journey to fix your physical and financial fitness is not going to be effortless. It will require attention and dedication. It will, in all respects, be a journey. Journeys always include ups and downs, learning and correction.

But having a plan will make your journey significantly easier. It will be the map and guide that keeps you on track when the going gets tough and seemingly impossible to navigate. Create a plan and stick to it, no matter what. Eventually, your plan will enable you to become more powerful than you ever imagined in your physical and financial fitness.

As you stick to the plans you make for yourself, you will inevitably earn credibility with yourself. That credibility is essential to building and retaining self-esteem. Self-esteem in turn is critical to your success in your financial and physical fitness. It has a snowball effect in all aspects of your life. Eventually, as you carry out the plans you make for yourself, you will become unstoppable.

In *How to make People Like You in 90 Seconds or Less*, author Nicholas Boothman offers a three part method intended to increase your ability to communicate well with others, entitled the "KFC" method.

The KFC method is the outline you will use to create plans and goals for yourself. The KFC method is as follows: first, you must **KNOW** what you want, then you must **FIND** out what you are getting, and finally, you must **CHANGE** what you are doing until you get what you want.[vii]

You must know what you want out of your physical and financial fitness. You will discover what you want by engaging in brainstorming sessions where you set forth all of the goals you wish to accomplish as they relate to your physical and financial fitness.

(1) Setting fitness and financial goals. (Knowing what you want.)

It would be difficult—even impossible— to design your dream house without first knowing what you want in a house. Likewise, it would be difficult to build your dream body or achieve financial success without first knowing what you want.

So, what do you want?

Take a moment in the space provided below or on your own paper to write down everything that you want out of your physical and financial fitness. Do not be afraid to dream big. After all, the only limitations on your dreams are the ones that you impose upon yourself. What is your ideal weight? Do you want to gain or lose weight? How much? Do you want to add muscle? Do you want to feel healthier? What about your financial goals? Do you want to get out of debt? Do you want to save for an early retirement? Do you wish to double your income? Do you want to triple it? Do you long for your dream home? A grand gap year where you travel the world? You can have anything that you want out of life, but it starts with developing concrete goals and dreams first.

List your biggest financial and physical fitness goals first. Then, set smaller goals that will help you achieve your larger goals. Again, do not let yourself be inhibited by the limits you might be placing on yourself. Write down your goals. As you write them down, allow yourself to feel excited about your goals. What would it be like to actually achieve that goal?

Dream big. You only have one life to live, so live the one you want.

When I was twelve years old, I drafted a bucket list of all the things I wanted to get out of life. A few things that made the list—I wanted to be a lawyer. I wanted to go skydiving. I wanted to live in Hawaii. I wanted to travel the world. I wanted children. After I wrote the list, I do not recall looking at it again until I was an adult, about to graduate law school and holding my newborn son in my arms. I had achieved nearly everything on that list, even though I did not even remember that the list existed.

I don't share this story so that you will conjure up a list of goals and dreams and then forget about it. The purpose of writing down your goals is that there is something wonderful and powerful about writing your dreams down. It plants ideas deep into our subconscious, allowing them to form into tangible, achievable ideas. Our subconscious has a way of helping us figure out *how* we can achieve our dreams by gifting us with new ideas. When you have an idea, write it down. And then act on it as swiftly as you can.

You do not have to come up with all of your goals and dreams all at once. As ideas come into your mind, add them to your list, even if it is days, weeks, months, or years later from your original draft. If you do not have enough space in the designated area below, use the space provided at the end of the book or you can write in your own journal or scrap paper. But keep these goals and dreams in a place where you will review them and where they will not be lost.

Include deadlines for each of your goals. For example, *I want to move into my dream house in the next ten years*. Give yourself concrete deadlines. If those deadlines come and go without the results you desired, set new deadlines and continue working towards those dreams. Do not give up. Do not allow anyone to make you feel small or feel that you cannot achieve what you desire. This includes you. Believe in yourself and your ability to achieve wonderful things in your physical and financial life. You might wonder, who am I to achieve these great things? But in reality, who aren't you to achieve greatness?

Prioritize your goals—after you have written down your financial goals, start making decisions on what goals you would like to accomplish first. For example, if a couple of your goals are to pay off all of your debt and another goal is to purchase a home, prioritize the debt repayment and then start saving up for a home. Always prioritize paying off debt above other financial goals. This will bring you peace of mind and enable you to achieve other financial goals. Indicate the priority order with a number next to each goal. For example, say you have goals of paying off credit card debt with high interest rates, paying off student loans, and saving for a down payment on a house, you could prioritize them like so:

Pay off credit card debt (1)
Pay off student loans (2)
Save for house (3)

MY GOALS:

(2) TAKE INVENTORY. (Figure out where you are.)

Once you have written down all of your goals and dreams, you must start figuring out exactly where you are financially and physically. After all, it would be extraordinarily difficult to achieve any goal without knowing where you stand. Figuring out where you are with your physical and financial fitness will help you figure out how to make the changes necessary to achieve your goals. Knowing where you are can be a painful and vulnerable task. But without that vulnerability, you cannot progress.

Accordingly, you will be taking inventory of all aspects of your physical and financial fitness. Taking inventory is an important part of any business. In fact, for most businesses that sell tangible products, it would be practically impossible to operate the business without taking inventory. How would you know how much product to order? How would you know how much money the business had? How would you know how much money to spend on business operations?

Run your fitness and your finances just like you would run a business. It is ok if you do not have experience with taking inventory. You can start now. We will take inventory periodically throughout this challenge, but the first part starts during Phase I. If you find it difficult to discover truths about yourself—maybe your weight is much higher than you anticipated, maybe there is more debt than you thought, maybe your waist line is thicker than you imagined—fret not. Simply by beginning this program, you are already on the right path to getting on track and getting your financial and physical fitness where you want them to be. Whatever you have done and wherever you are, it is never too late to start changing your behavior.

FITNESS INVENTORY:

To start your fitness inventory you will weigh yourself, take your measurements, and calculate your BMI. Each of these measurements should be considered together and not individually. For example, your weight or BMI individually might not accurately portray how physically fit you are. You could hypothetically be on the heavy side and have a high BMI because you are muscular. On the other hand, you could also be heavy because your body consists of a higher percentage of body fat. Similarly, your waist might measure small, but you may have excess weight on your hips and thighs that if removed, would lead you to a healthier life. The same applies to the calculation of your BMI. Be honest with yourself. Use these measurements to get an idea of where you are so that you can make the changes you need to get where you want to go.

You will take each of these measurements at the beginning, middle, and end of the program to calculate your progress.

Weigh yourself

Phase I: _____

Phase III: _____

Final: _____

Measure waist

Phase I: _____

Phase III: _____

Final: _____

Calculate your BMI

Phase I: _____

Phase III: _____

Final: _____

FINANCIAL INVENTORY

Taking financial inventory will be a little more involved than your physical fitness inventory and will, in some respects, be done on a weekly basis. Inventory will include: tracking your expenses, tallying up all of your debts, tallying up all sources of income, and checking your credit score.

Financial Inventory:

- *Start tracking all of your expenses, immediately.*
- *Tally up ALL of your debts.*
- *Tally up income from every source.*
- *Check your credit score.*

I. *Tracking Expenses*

You need a clear picture of exactly what your expenses are if you are to improve your financial situation. You need to know where all of your money is going every month.

There are a couple of ways that you can track your expenses. First, there is the good old-fashioned way of saving your receipts and bills and sitting down to calculate them. Another option is to download an app to your smartphone that tracks your expenses. There are a number of free apps that you can download that make it easy to track your expenses. They will require you to enter in all of your bank account information, credit cards, and other debts.

I like to combine both methods. I use an app but I also periodically sit down and write down every expense I have each month. If you have another effective method, feel free to use that. Choose any method you prefer. The point is simply to tally up every expense that you have. You will do this throughout the remainder of the program, checking in every week at your weekly meeting (more on the weekly meeting later) to see what you have spent.

Remember to include any of your irregular expenses, such as those expenses that are not monthly. For example, you might annually or semi-annually make a car insurance payment. If that is the case, add up the total sum you pay for the year and divide it by twelve (for twelve months in the year, six if it is semi-annually). I have several payments that fall in this category, such as various forms of insurance that I carry. All you need to do is calculate how much it costs per month by totaling the sum and dividing it by twelve.

In addition, be sure to include any monthly debt payments

that you are required to make. And most importantly, include a savings percentage among your expenses. An ideal minimum savings goal would be 10% of your income. If you can afford to save more, do so. If 10% is too difficult right now given your current income and current expenses, opt for something lower—even as low as one percent. The point is to get you in the habit of paying yourself first.

Pay yourself first.

You may have heard of the concept of paying yourself first, but what does this mean exactly? It means that before you pay ANY debts or other bills that you owe, you should pay yourself. Before you get too excited, this does NOT mean that you get to start spending money on yourself first. It means that you have a savings account or other designated place for your money to go. When you get paid, the first thing you do is deposit the money into that account.

Does this idea seem counterintuitive to you? Well, it shouldn't. You are the most important person on your payroll. If you are ever going to meet any of your financial goals, you must get into the habit of paying yourself first, even if you have to start small.

There are many benefits to paying yourself first. The most obvious, of course, is that you will have the money you need to meet your financial goals. There are also psychological benefits—you earn credibility with yourself. You can trust yourself to do the things that you say you are going to do— like paying off debt, saving for retirement, or saving up money for any other purpose. You practice the art of self-control (more on this in Phase IV) and when we exercise self-control, we feel good about ourselves.

So what exactly will do with these savings? Simple. You will direct them towards the financial goals that you listed above. That might mean that you use the money to make extra debt payments for an aggressive debt repayment goal. For example, one of our financial goals was to get out of $600k of student loan debt as quickly as possible. Any extra money that we had went straight towards this goal, at the expense of any of our other goals because the interest was so toxic to us. Another example is that you might be saving up for a down payment on a house. That money would go into a savings account and stay there until you have enough for the down payment. Whatever your priority goal is, direct the money towards the goal. As you achieve those goals, move on and direct the money to your next priority goal.

A final note: when you are listing your expenses, you may find, as I did, that it is difficult to recall every single expense you have. Do your best to create the most comprehensive list that you can. As additional expenses come to your awareness, come back and add them to your list.

MY MONTHLY EXPENSES:

II. Tally up all of your debts.

It is hard to know where you are financially and how you can improve without knowing how much money you currently do or do not have. To find this out, you must add up all of your debts.

You may find this to be a painful exercise. But nothing will motivate you more than having a sound understanding of your financial situation. Sit down and create a list of every dollar that you owe, and organize it in a list in priority order. List those debts with the highest earning interest first down to the lowest earning interest debts. You will prioritize them this way so that you will know which debts you should eliminate first. Debts that earn the highest interest should be eliminated before lower-earning interest debts for the obvious reason that higher-earning interest debts are more expensive. Many interest-bearing loans compound interest daily. If you have a significant amount of debt with high-earning interest, this can bury you financially. Eliminate those debts first, and then work towards becoming debt free with your lower-earning interest debts.

One rule of thumb is that you should pay off debt aggressively if it earns higher interest than it would earn if it were an investment. For example, if you have credit card debt that earns twelve percent interest, you should pay off that debt before investing in something like a mutual fund that boasts eight percent interest. To give you an idea of a good return on an investment, according to data acquired by Morningstar[viii] over an eighty year period, people who invested in small and large company stocks received a return on investment between nine and twelve percent. For many people, it is much lower. Of course with any investment, you run a risk of losing money. For most people, it is a good idea to keep things simple and get rid of debt before investing.

PHASED STARTING TOTAL DEBT:

_____

PHASED ENDING TOTAL DEBT:

_____

DEBT ENTITY AND AMOUNT (ex: Chase Bank, $15,000)	Interest Rate (ex: 7.9%)

III. Add up your income from every source.

Add up income that you receive from any source. Include money from anyone with whom you share money, side hustles like income from rental property, cash back offers that you receive, or selling products online that brings in additional income, even occasionally. Every dollar should be accounted for. Remember, are you running your personal finances as you would run a business? Pretend that you are being audited.

In the next phase, you will create a budget. One thing that set my family back from creating a budget in our early years was the fact that our income was highly irregular. It made it difficult to calculate an average income that we felt we could live off of. In reality, this should have been of no consequence to us. If you have irregular income (for example, perhaps you work at an hourly wage and cannot put in consistent hours since you are in school, or perhaps you are in sales and earn a commission) simply count your irregular income based on the lowest earning income month of the year. If you are a student living off of student loans, divide the lump sum you are given at the beginning of the semester to live off of by the number of months you have to live off of it. (P.S. if you are a student, do everything you can to spend far less than what you are given.) Do your best to report your income to yourself as accurately as possible. You will work out the kinks as you create a budget in the weeks to come.

IV. Check your credit score.

It is generally recommended that you check your credit score once per year. If you haven't checked yours in the last six months, go ahead and check it. Even if you suspect that you have excellent credit, you should check your score once per year to make sure that it is where you think it is and that your identity has not been stolen.

You can request a free copy of your credit report from each of the three major credit-reporting agencies (Equifax, Experian, and TransUnion) once each year at www.annualcreditreport.com or by calling 1-877-322-8228.

Generally speaking (there is some disagreement from different sources here), a score of 800 or above is considered excellent. A score of 700 or above is considered good. A score between 600-700 is fair and anything below 600 is considered poor.

Note that having good credit is not everything. You can have an excellent credit score and be in terrible shape financially. Look at your finances holistically. Credit scores improve based on how many lines of credit you have open and how diligent you are at making payments among other things. You could hypothetically have thousands of dollars in debt but have excellent credit. For example, when I paid off my student loans, my credit score actually went down because I no longer had that line of credit open. I had a better credit score when I had more debt. That seems silly, doesn't it? While you should aim for a good credit score, it should not be at the expense of opening more lines of credit or otherwise obtaining new debt.

MY CREDIT SCORE IS _____

3) CHANGE YOUR BEHAVIOR

Now that you know what you want, having set out clear defined goals and assessed precisely where your fitness and finances are, you can more clearly see what changes you need to make to achieve your goals.

You can earn the things that you want. Start identifying what changes you will need to make in order to accomplish your goals. For example, perhaps one of your goals is to kick your daily coffee habit. Upon taking inventory of your expenses, you realize that your stop at the coffee shop is costing you about $6 per day. You have a financial goal of saving $300 per month—cutting out that stop alone will put you more than half way towards your goal.

Now, take the time to brainstorm behaviors that you can change that will help you reach your health and financial goals. Resolve to make the changes that you need to succeed. You will probably find two things: 1) some things will be really easy to give up and make a big difference in making strides towards achieving your goals and 2) some behaviors will be quite difficult to change to get you on track to achieve your goals. Do those things anyway. Review your goals. Allow yourself to spend time imaging what it would feel like to achieve your goals. Remember what is actually most important to you, and act accordingly.

Changes I can make to help me achieve my goals:

"By failing to prepare, you are preparing to fail."
— Benjamin Franklin

<u>PHASE I SUMMARY OF TASKS</u>

Weekly meal planning

Weekly money meetings

Phase I workouts

Set fitness and financial goals

Take Inventory

Check credit score

PHASE I WORKOUTS

WEEK 1:

DAY 1: LEGS
    CARDIO: 20 MINUTES (FASTED)
    STRENGTH:
        LUNGE KICKS 5X20 (PER LEG) FOR SPEED
        SQUATS 5X20 FOR SPEED
        LYING LEG CURL 5X15
        JUMP SQUATS 5X20
        100 CRUNCHES
    CARDIO: 20 MINUTES

DAY 2: CARDIO: 40 MINUTES (LIGHT)

DAY 3: CHEST AND TRICEPS
    CARDIO: 20 MINUTES (FASTED)
    STRENGTH:
        CHEST FLYS 4X10
        PUSH UPS 3X10
        STANDING ONE ARM FLYS 2X12, PER ARM
        TRICEPS PULL DOWN 3X12
        LYING TRICEPS PULL DOWN 3X12
        TRICEP DIPS 3X12
        100 RUSSIAN TWISTS

DAY 4: BACK AND BICEPS
    CARDIO: 20 MINUTES (FASTED)
    STRENGTH:
        UNDERHAND PULL UPS 4X10
        CHIN UPS 4X10
        BOW POSE 3X12
        STRAIGHT ARM PULL DOWN 7X20
        CONCENTRATION CURLS 4X15 PER ARM
        CURLS 3X12 PER ARM
        100 RUSSIAN TWISTS

CARDIO: 20 MINUTES
DAY 5: SHOULDERS ABS AND CALVES
    CARDIO: 20 MINUTES (FASTED)
    STRENGTH:
        SHOULDER PUSHUPS 4X15
        SIDE LATERAL RAISES 5X20
        SHOULDER ROWS 5X20
        WEIGHTED SIT UPS 5X20
        LYING LEG THRUSTS 3X15
  CALF RAISES 5X20
    CARDIO 20 MINUTES
DAY 6: LEGS
    CARDIO: 20 MINUTES
    STRENGTH:
        SUPERSET:
            2X30 JUMPING LUNGES (15 PER SIDE)
            ALTERNATING WITH
            2X20 LYING LEG CURLS
        SUPERSET:
            3X40 WALKING LUNGES ALTERNATING
            WITH
            3X15 LEG CURLS (PER LEG)
        SQUATS 3X50
        3X40 WALKING LUNGES
        3X20 DONKEY KICKS
DAY 7: CARDIO: 40 MINUTES (LIGHT)

WEEK 2

DAY 1: CHEST AND TRICEPS
  CARDIO: 20 MINUTES (FASTED)
  STRENGTH:
      CHEST FLYS 5X10
      PUSHUPS 2X MAX REPS
      STANDING ONE ARM FLYS 2X10 PER ARM
      TRICEPS PULL DOWN 3X10
      LYING TRICEPS PULL DOWN 3X10
      STANDING TRICEPS EXTENSION 3X10
      100 RUSSIAN TWISTS
  CARDIO: 20 MIN

DAY 2: CARDIO: 40 MINUTES

DAY 3: LEGS
  CARDIO: 20 MINUTES (FASTED)
  STRENGTH:
      LUNGE KICKS 5X15 PER LEG
      SQUATS 5X20 FOR SPEED
      LYING LEG CURL 5X15
      JUMP SQUATS 5X20
      100 CRUNCHES
  CARDIO: 20 MINUTES

DAY 4: CARDIO: 40 MINUTES (LIGHT)

DAY 5: BACK AND BICEPS
  CARDIO: 20 MINUTES (FASTED)
  STRENGTH:
      UNDERHAND PULL UPS, 4X10
      ROWS 4X12
      LOCUST POSE 3X12 PULSE
      STRAIGHT ARM PULL DOWN 7X15
      CONCENTRATION CURLS 4X15 (PER ARM)
      CURLS 3X15 (PER ARM)

100 RUSSIAN TWISTS

CARDIO: 20 MINUTES

DAY 6: SHOULDERS ABS AND CALVES

CARDIO: 20 MINUTES (FASTED)

STRENGTH:

SHOULDER PUSH UPS 4X20

SIDE LATERAL RAISES 4X20

UPRIGHT ROWS 3X15

REAR DELT RAISE 7X15

CRUNCHES 3X20

CALF RAISES, 6X20

CARDIO: 20 MINUTES

DAY 7: LEGS

CARDIO: 20 MINUTES

STRENGTH:

SUPERSET:

JUMPING LUNGES 2X30 (15 PER SIDE)

ALTERNATING WITH

LYING LEG CURLS 2X20

SUPERSET:

WALKING LUNGES 3X40

ALTERNATING WITH

LYING LEG CURLS 3X15

SQUATS 3X50

WALKING LUNGES 1X40

DONKEY KICKS 2X20 (PER LEG)

PHASE II

THE ART OF HOPEFULNESS

"Life has no limit, if you're not afraid to get in it."
-   Mason Jennings

Two travelers visited a village high in the mountains. The first traveler journeyed from the village in the mountains to a village in the valley. On his way down, there was a monk, working in a field.

"I am going to the village in the valley," he said. "Can you tell me what it is like?"

The monk stopped his work for a moment, and asked, 'Where have you come from?"

"I have been in the village in the mountains," the traveler responded.

The monk asked, "What was it like?"

"Awful!" replied the traveler. "They didn't speak my language, the food was strange, and I had to sleep on the floor for there were no beds."

The monk said, "Then I think you will find that the village in the valley is much the same."

Later, the second traveler journeyed from the village in the mountains and saw the same monk on the side of the road. "I am going to the village in the valley!" said he. "Can you tell me what it is like?

The monk stopped his work for a moment, and asked, 'Where have you come from?"

"I have been in the village in the mountains," the traveler responded.

The monk asked, "What was it like?"

"Wonderful! I was able to learn a new language, try new foods, and sleep on the floor—I hadn't tried that before. I tried new things and met wonderful people. It was a beautiful, unforgettable experience," replied the traveler.

The monk said, "Then I think you will find that the village in the valley is much the same."[ix]

The two travelers in this story were given the same experience and yet their takeaways were markedly different. There are a few lessons to be learned from this story. One important lesson is that it is not so much what happens to you in life but how you respond to it that makes a difference. You have a choice to learn and grow from new and difficult experiences. Each traveler was exposed to new foods, lifestyles, and languages that they had not experienced. The second traveler celebrated this fact and took the opportunity to learn and grow. The other crooned at the experience and learned nothing. Your task with your physical and financial fitness is to be like the second traveler. Look for opportunities to learn and grow. Put a positive outlook on your life. If you have experienced setbacks with your finances or physical health, your reaction to those setbacks is what will make you successful (or not).

To succeed financially and physically, master the art of hopefulness. Said differently, become optimistic about your physical and financial fitness.

Everyone, on some level, desires physical and financial health. One of the most important secrets to achieve either of these is to become optimistic about yourself and your life— especially regarding your financial and physical fitness. Thus, the second phase of this program will teach you the importance of controlling your thinking in specific ways that will enable you to feel happy no matter what your situation is.

There is no shortage of reasons why you should use the power of positive thinking in your life. Optimists enjoy better health. Optimists live longer. Optimists get promoted faster and receive more job offers. Optimists enjoy less stress. Having an optimistic outlook increases productivity. Optimism aids in achieving goals. Optimists are resilient. Optimists take responsibility for their actions—they learn from their setbacks and as a result are more successful. In addition, optimists view setbacks as isolated incidents. As such, can you see how mastering the art of hopefulness will help you achieve financial and physical success?

But, even if you accept that an optimistic outlook is going to aid you not only in this program but also throughout your life, how do you learn to have an optimistic outlook?

In this Phase, you will learn how to control your thinking so that you feel joyful about yourself and your situation no matter what you have done, what has happened to you, what you will do, or what will happen to you in life.

Hopefulness Training

The first step toward becoming a more optimistic person is to make the *choice* to become one. Then, you must continue to make that choice each time you are presented with an opportunity to be optimistic. This is *hopefulness training*. Hopefulness is not only a habit. It is an art. Like most art forms, it will take practice to master. Practice starts now.

The next step is resolving to not waste energy on anything that is outside of your control. This includes things like traffic, natural disasters, your own genetics, and what other people say and do. Instead, harbor energy into things that you can control—how much and intense you work out, sticking to a budget, working hard at work, and the like. In order to succeed in your personal finances and your physical health, you must not waste energy on things you cannot control. Focus on what you can control and keep a positive outlook in all things.

The third step in hopefulness is training is to not get set back by setbacks. Understand that there will be situations and seasons in life when things might not go the way you desire or expect. Some people who are trying to view things with a positive outlook may feel foolish when things do not go well. They may become disheartened and cynical. True optimists are aware that they live in an imperfect world in which love ends, dreams are shattered, and people are cheated; however, they still hold fast to a positive outlook.

To be sure, at some point life will hand you a setback or two—or ten. One month, your car might break down and it might completely destroy your budget. Or, you might experience heartbreak and go on a binge of overeating for a day or two. Your job is not to go completely berserk over the setback. Instead, only worry about how you will use that setback to your advantage. Learn from it, and get back on track. Have faith in yourself that you can. Give yourself time to grieve and be kind to yourself, but keep a positive long-term outlook on life.

Resolve to think like an optimist, no matter what happens to you in life. You may not be able to control every event, but you can control the way you react to every event. Controlling your reaction is everything. Being able to control your reaction ultimately gives control back to you and helps you control future events. Remember that failure breeds success because of the lessons it teaches. Learn from your failures and setbacks so that you can be successful.

In addition to the three steps of practicing the art of hopefulness training, you will develop a mantra to help keep your thoughts positive.

DEVELOP A MANTRA

My two-year-old son went through a phase where he would cry "I can't, I can't" over any task that he could not immediately accomplish. For example, he did this when putting his books away on the shelf when the shelf was too high to reach. He created high expectations for himself—if he could not do a task exactly the way he saw my husband or I perform it, he would become powerfully frustrated.

As a parent, this was heartbreaking to observe. Of course no two year old should perform tasks on the same level as an adult. On one such occasion, we were painting. He asked me to paint a fire truck. When he tried to copy it and did not get a similar result, he threw himself on the ground and cried "I can't I can't!"

It occurred to me that, as his parent, it was my responsibility to teach him that he *could*. He might not be able to make a perfect fire truck on his first try, but over time, if he practiced, he would be able to do it. But I needed to explain in quick, simple terms that over time, he would learn how to form rectangles and add shapes together to form other objects, such as a firetruck. As he imagined something, he could learn to draw it out with time and practice.

Instead of delving into those specifics, I taught him the simple principle behind what I wanted him to understand. I scooped him up in my arms, held him close and said, "You CAN do hard things." I didn't say anything else, I just held him until he was ready to get down.

The next day, he was stacking up some blocks. They kept falling over. He cried, "I can't! I can't!" as he often did, and threw himself down on the ground, defeated. I scooped him up and repeated what we had done the day before. "You CAN do hard things."

Over the course of about a week, this continued under various circumstances. He would get frustrated; I would pick him up, and remind him he could do hard things.

And then one day, as I was cooking dinner, I heard him in the next room putting away his books. They kept falling off the shelf. He became frustrated. He said "I can't, I..." and then he stopped. He got really excited, and his little legs pitter-pattered across our hardwood floor all the way to me in the kitchen where he loudly proclaimed, "I CAN DO HARD THINGS! COME LOOK MOMMA!"

I followed him to where his bookshelf was, and we put away

the books together as he continued to giggle and tell me how he could do hard things. He was right.

"I can do hard things" became my son's personal mantra. He still repeats it often. I hope it sticks with him throughout his life.

Just like my son's personal mantra helped him shake off negative feelings about his abilities, during Phase II, you will develop your own personal mantra to help you shake off any negativity that may sneak its way into your life.

To begin this task, take time and consider some of the things that you struggle with most. Do you struggle with self-worth? Are you easily distracted? Are you an emotionally responsive person? (For example, do you spend money or overeat when you are trying to make yourself feel better?) What is it that seems to weigh you down the most?

I, for one, am an easily distracted person. At any given time, I will have MANY projects going on. And I often jump around from task to task. This makes it difficult to accomplish anything. I might get a little accomplished on each project, but it means that each project takes *forever* to complete. To establish my point, I started writing this section on what my mantra was. I then remembered something that I needed to share with you later in the book. I jumped to that section and started writing. Then, the buzzer went off on my laundry, and I went to take things out of the dryer. Before I knew it, I was folding clothes and starting to clean my house. Then I remembered one of my many personal mantras— "One task at a time!" I repeated it to myself several times and came back to complete this section.

And that is precisely how your mantra should operate to serve you in your daily life. Your mantra should help you get out of whatever funk you are in, feel better about yourself, and keep chugging along.

You, of course, can develop several mantras if you wish. You can start by writing one now, and come back later to edit your mantra or create additional ones as you have time to ponder.

Some ideas: "I am enough." "Hard work pays off." "Faith over fear."

My mantra is:

DEVELOP A STATEMENT OF PURPOSE

After developing one or more personal mantras, you will develop a statement of purpose, to help keep your mind focused on your goals. It can be as simple as "I want to gain money and lose weight." The reason for this statement? You become what you think about most. Napoleon Hill said, "We are what we are because of the vibrations of thought which we pluck up and register through the stimuli of our daily environment.[x]" Thus, you want a message that you can repeat every day (in addition to your mantra) that will help you build faith in yourself. Create a statement that will stimulate a positive vibration of thought. Most successful companies have mission statements. These companies base most if not all of their company-wide decisions on their mission statement. For example, one of Nike's mission statements is "Bring inspiration and innovation to every athlete in the world." If Nike was brainstorming product development and someone inside the company pitched an idea to start selling art kits, Nike would likely reject this idea, since art kits do not bring inspiration and innovation to their athletes. It is not a part of their brand or who they are.

So who are you? What is your "brand"? What vibrations of thought do you want entering your mind every day? What do you want to become? What do you want to achieve? Choose something positive.

SLAY THE DRAGON

Your final task in Phase II is to *slay the dragon*. This is a technique that is sometimes used in therapy designed to help clients let go of negative emotions and memories they are having a hard time letting go of.

Holding on to negative emotions has harmful consequences, sometimes causing very intense, life-crippling impairment. These harbored emotions can bring you deep sadness, which can then spiral into depression and anxiety. Negative emotions can make you physically ill. They can influence other relationships in your life. And they certainly can impact your physical and financial fitness. An underlying goal of this program is to find and overcome problems that are at the root of your physical and financial problems. When you are able to overcome the root problems, it is easier to avoid falling into old, poor financial and fitness habits. Slaying the dragon (letting go of negative life events) will help you overcome your negative emotions so that you can work on being a better, more successful version of you.

So what is slaying the dragon? First and foremost, it is a metaphor—an effective mechanism that you can use to change stubborn unconscious negative thoughts and emotions. Your metaphorical dragon is whatever you struggle with most, especially pertaining to your finances or physical fitness. You might not readily know what your dragon is. You will discover it through this exercise.

Start by writing down every negative feeling you have about your physical and financial fitness. It can be *anything*—as long as it is a negative feeling that you desire to be free from. Do you think you are fat? Do you wish you had more money? Do you feel stressed about how much debt is weighing you down? Do you have too many expenses in your life? Is your mortgage drowning you? Are you stressed about not having enough money saved for retirement? Has someone offended you in regards to your finances or physical fitness? Did they make a hurtful comment? Whatever it is—write it down. And write down all of your feelings associated with those negative thoughts.

For example: *When our crippling student loan payments became due, I started losing sleep at night. I wasn't sure how we were going to make our payments each month. I started overeating during the day to cope with that stress. I started feeling more stress about overeating because it costs money and I was gaining weight. I knew it was impacting my health. Now, I feel fat and gross. I feel helpless. I feel guilty about taking the time to work out when I could be working more hours or doing things to make more payments on my student loans. I feel jealous of my close friends who are very secure financially. Many of them are stay-at-home moms who get to spend a lot of time with their kids. Sarah asked me how I could stand to work and miss out on all my time with my kids. That offended me. My husband doesn't make as much money as hers does. I don't have the option to not work. We have too much debt. I already felt guilty about being away from my kids before she said that. In truth, I somehow both don't really like her but also I feel jealous of her.*

Don't give yourself any word limit. Sometimes I do this exercise and it fills ten pages, and sometimes all I need are a few sentences. When you have completed writing down every negative feeling you have associated with your thoughts, you will do one of two things: 1) you may shred the papers into tiny pieces and throw them away, or 2) you may burn the paper until it is completely unrecognizable. Really, you can destroy it in any manner that best suits you, but make sure that it is completely destroyed. This is metaphorically slaying the dragon. As you destroy the paper containing all of your negative feelings, imagine yourself letting go of each and every negative emotion. Take time to relish in the feeling of lifting that burden out of your life.

You don't have to navigate through every single negative feeling you have ever had in one sitting. You can do this over several exercises of slaying the dragon. I like to perform this activity once per week to make sure that I am not letting sneaky little negative dragons creep their way back into my life.

After practicing this activity, you will be free from the negative emotions that have held you back in the past. And as little dragons creep their way back into your life, which they will inevitably do, simply perform this exercise again and again.

PHASE II SUMMARY OF TASKS

Weekly meal planning

Weekly money meetings

Phase II workouts

Develop a mantra

Create a statement of purpose

Practice slaying the dragon at least once

PHASE II WORKOUTS

WEEK 3

DAY 1: ABS, CHEST, AND TRICEPS

INCLINE PUSHUPS 3X12, 1 MINUTE RUN IN PLACE BETWEEN SETS

DECLINE PUSHUPS 3X12, 1 MINUTE MOUNTAIN CLIMBERS BETWEEN SETS

PUSHUPS 3X12, 1 MINUTE JUMPING JACKS BETWEEN SETS

TRICEP DIPS 4X15, 1 MINUTE JUMPING SQUATS BETWEEN SETS

CRUNCHES 4X20

PLATINUM PLANKS

HOLD FOR 45 SECONDS THEN DIRECTLY INTO SIDE PLANK 45 SECONDS PER SIDE

DAY 2: LEGS AND SHOULDERS

SHOULDER PRESS 4X12, 1 MINUTE HIGH KNEES BETWEEN SETS

ALTERNATING SHOULDER PRESS 3X12, 1 MINUTE BUTT KICKS BETWEEN SETS

UPRIGHT ROWS 3X12, 1 MINUTE SPRINT

JUMP SQUATS 4X15, 1 MIUTE JUMPING LUNGES, ALTERNATING LEGS

DEADLIGHTS 4X12, 1 MINUTE MOUNTAIN CLIMBERS

WALKING LUNGES 4X20 PER LEG, 1 MINUTE OF FRONT KICKS

CALF RAISES 6X20 REPS

DAY 3: BACK AND BICEPS

CARDIO: 20 MINUTES (FASTED)

STANDING ROWS 4X12, 1 MINUTE BUTT KICKS BETWEEN SETS

WIDE GRIP PULL UPS (PULL UP BAR OR BANDS) 4X12 MODIFIED AS NEEDED, 1 MINUTE HIGH KNEES BETWEEN SETS

UNDERARM PULL UPS (PULL UP BAR OR BANDS) 4X12 MODIFIED AS NEEDED, 1 MINUTE LATERAL HOPS BETWEEN SETS

BICEP CURLS 4X12, 1 MINUTE MOUNTAIN CLIMBERS BETWEEN SETS

SUPERMAN POSE 4X15, 1 MINUTE BOX JUMPS (OR KNEE TUCKS) BETWEEN SETS

DAY 4: CARDIO: 30 MINUTES

DAY 5: ABS, CHEST, AND TRICEPS

INCLINE PUSHUPS 3X12, 1 MINUTE RUN IN PLACE BETWEEN SETS

DECLINE PUSHUPS 3X12, 1 MINUTE MOUNTAIN CLIMBERS BETWEEN SETS

PUSHUPS 3X12, 1 MINUTE JUMPING JACKS BETWEEN SETS

TRICEP DIPS 4X15, 1 MINUTE JUMPING SQUATS BETWEEN SETS

CRUNCHES 4X20

PLATINUM PLANKS

HOLD FOR 45 SECONDS THEN DIRECTLY INTO SIDE PLANK 45 SECONDS PER SIDE

CARDIO: 20 MINUTES

DAY 6: LEGS AND SHOULDERS

SHOULDER PRESS 4X12, 1 MINUTE HIGH KNEES BETWEEN SETS

ALTERNATING SHOULDER PRESS 3X12, 1 MINUTE BUTT KICKS BETWEEN SETS

UPRIGHT ROWS 3X12, 1 MINUTE SPRINT

JUMP SQUATS 4X15, 1 MIUTE JUMPING LUNGES, ALTERNATING LEGS

DEADLIGHTS 4X12, 1 MINUTE MOUNTAIN CLIMBERS

WALKING LUNGES 4X20 PER LEG, 1 MINUTE OF FRONT KICKS

CALF RAISES 6X20 REPS

DAY 7: REST

WEEK 4

DAY 1: LEGS

    LUNGE KICKS 4x20 (PER LEG)

    SUMO SQUATS 4x20

    HORSE KICKS + FIRE HYDRANT 4x20 OF EACH

    WALKING LUNGES 4x20

    WALL SIT 60 SECONDS

    30 SECOND REST BETWEEN EACH, REPEAT THE SET UNTIL YOU CAN'T

DAY 2: CARDIO: 40 MINUTES

DAY 3: CHEST & TRICEPS

    20 PUSH UPS

    20 CHAIR TRICEP DIPS

    20 PLANK TO TRICEP PUSH UPS (20 SECOND PLANK, THEN TRICEP PUSHUP)

    20 DECLINE PUSH UPS

    10 BURPEES

    30 SECOND REST BETWEEN EACH, REPEAT SET UNTIL YOU CAN'T

DAY 4: SHOULDERS & ABS

    CARDIO: 20 MINUTES (FASTED)

    SHOULDER PUSHUPS 4x20

    1 MINUTEPLANK

    SIDE LATERAL RAISES 4X20

    UPRIGHT ROWS 3X15

    REAR DELT RAISES 7X15

    CRUNCHES 3X25

    CALF RAISES 6X20

DAY 5: CARDIO: 40 MINUTES

DAY 6: BACK (rest as needed during and between each exercise)

    20 UNDERHAND PULL UPS

    20 CHIN UPS

    20 WIDE GRIP PULL UPS

    2O PULSES LOCUST POSE

    REPEAT UNTIL YOU CAN'T

DAY 7: REST

PHASE III

ABILITY

"Success is the maximum utilization of the *ability* that you have."
- Zig Zigler

"If it is to be, it is up to me."
- Brian Tracy

A man and his friend walked to work together every day. Every day, they passed by a neighbor. And every day, the man greeted the neighbor with a cheery "good morning." The neighbor responded the same way every morning—with a scowl.

When the friend had enough of the neighbor's curtness, he asked, "Why do you continue to say hello to that crabby man?" The cheerful man gave a thoughtful reply. "Why should I let him decide how I am going to act?"[xi]

To succeed in your physical and financial fitness, you must learn to take responsibility for the things that happen to you. The man in this story could have easily let his grumpy neighbor's attitude get the best of him. It would have been easy to respond back with curtness or to ignore the neighbor. But the man did not let the neighbor decide what kind of person he was going to be. Instead, he took control of the situation. He did not allow his circumstances to control the outcome of his life.

Just like the man did not let outside influences control his actions, so you should act with your finances and fitness. No matter what has happened to put you in whatever physical or financial situation you are in, you must learn to accept it, own it, learn from it, and move on. Take time to carefully think about how you can react to your situation to improve it.

In the third phase of this program you will master the *ability* that exists within you to succeed in your financial and physical fitness. In *7 Habits of Highly Effective People*, Stephen Covey offered a simple yet profound definition of the word responsible. He strategically separated the word into **response - able**. He postulated that, you, as a human being capable of rational thought, are ABLE to RESPOND. You have the **ability** to respond to the things that happen to and around you. You can't control everything that happens to you, but you are in complete control of *how* you respond. You are capable of making the choice to use the things that happen to you as stepping stones to success.

You are the only person in control of your life. You cannot always control what happens to you, but you can control the outcome of what happens based on how you **respond**. And you are **able** to respond simply because of who you are. That ability is inside of you. You have talents and gifts that are unique to you that will aid you in your response to those things that occur around you and influence you. You have the ability to succeed in both finances and physical fitness. You must channel that ability and choose how you will respond to the obstacles that you face.

Your first task in Phase III is to create a budget that will actually work for you. Your second task will be to increase your income so that you can meet your financial goals. These tasks are designed to refine your ability to respond to financial obstacles that you face.

CREATE A BUDGET

It may seem odd to you that you are now four weeks into this program and have not created a budget yet. That changes in this phase. Creating and living within a budget are two of the most important things you can do to achieve financial success. *Everyone* needs a budget. And I mean *everyone*. This includes starving college students, trust-fund families, blue-collar workers, and everyone in between.

Anyone can create a budget—but the key is to create a budget that will actually work for you. The budget you create now will hopefully be different than any others you have created in past that have inevitably fallen by the wayside.

You will run your own finances just as a successful business would run its finances. Imagine a big business operating without a financial plan. The business would not count how much money it had coming in. It wouldn't account for expenditures. It would act on a whim with how much inventory to purchase. It seems absurd, doesn't it? Things would quickly become chaotic. The business would no doubt find trouble at tax season and would have an extraordinarily difficult time becoming profitable. It would be practically impossible to make important decisions without knowing what financial resources the business did or did not have. Ultimately, such a poorly operated company would likely go out of business because money is the blood that keeps a business going. Successful companies account for every dollar.

Just like a successful business must keep track of every dollar, you too must account for every dollar that enters your household. Every dollar should have a purpose. You should know precisely how much money is coming in and precisely where it is going.

And this is precisely the reason we have waited a few weeks to tackle creating a budget. Because to create a *successful* budget takes time and knowledge of where you and your family stand financially—a fairly complete understanding of how much money comes into your household, how many expenses your household incurs, and where you can make changes, among other things. It is not a quick and easy fix. It is a problem that takes a little bit of work and manipulating and molding over time.

HOW TO CREATE A SUCCESSFUL BUDGET:

STEP 1: GATHER ALL OF YOUR EXPENSES THAT YOU LISTED IN PHASE I AND CREATE CATEGORIES. SET GOALS WITHIN EACH CATEGORY.

In Phase I, you tallied up all of your expenses. Recall that this included irregular expenses that you might only incur a few times a year or less. It also included putting away a percentage of your income to pay yourself FIRST after you receive a paycheck, before you pay any of your other expenses.

After you have an idea of what you are spending, categorize

your budget accordingly. You may have naturally done this when you originally listed your expenses. Examples of categories of your budget are: rent/mortgage, groceries, household items, gas, electricity, utilities, clothes, school supplies, car maintenance, and home repair.

With an idea of how much you are spending in each category, your next task is to set a goal for how much you will spend in each category. For example, you might set goals like:

Mortgage/rent: $1000
Groceries: $400
Utilities: $150
Car Maintenance and Gas: $200
Clothes: $50

Don't forget to include categories for the financial goals you created in Phase I.

STEP 2: GATHER ALL INCOME YOU TALLIED IN PHASE I AND MAKE SURE YOUR BUDGET GOALS ARE DIFFICULT BUT ATTAINABLE.

In addition to gathering all of your expenses, gather up all sources of income. Recall that any irregular income should be included in this list. If you are paid irregularly, (for example, if you are in sales and paid on commission) use your lowest earning month as the standard).

With a clear idea of what your income is, make sure that your budget goals are attainable. A good goal will cause you to stretch, but will not be impossible to attain. You must to have enough money for the whole month for every category in your budget.

STEP 3: GATHER ALL OF YOUR FINANCIAL GOALS FROM PHASE I.

If you have written your financial goals outside of this book, make sure you have them handy as you begin to create your budget. You will need to access your financial goals so that you can assess how much money you can direct to these goals from both the income that you pay yourself first and through any additional income left after all of your expenses are paid. This will also help inspire you to cut or reduce expenses from your budget that are not as important to you as your financial goals.

STEP 4: SUBTRACT EXPENSES FROM YOUR INCOME

Subtract all of your expenses from your income. Make sure that there is enough money for every category of your budget. Do some adjusting to your goals for each category as needed. You may have to reduce your budget in certain areas or eliminate non-essential categories all together. A non-essential category would be a category such as "eating out," or any other discretionary fund. These funds should be reduced or eliminated first, before essential funds like car or home maintenance, mortgage payment, or other payments that cannot be reduced.

In the coming task, you will work to increase income as needed to aid you in meeting each category, thereby increasing your non-essential categorical funds.

STEP 5: DIRECT ANY EXTRA MONEY TO SERVE YOUR FINANCIAL GOALS.

If there is any additional money left over after you have subtracted your expenses from income, direct it toward meeting your financial goals. Note that this is in *addition* to paying yourself first using a percentage of your income each month. Every dollar from your income should have purpose and intention.

If, on the other hand, you find after Step 4 that you don't have any more money to meet your financial goals, then you need to either find places in your budget where you can cut expenses, or you must increase your income to meet those needs. You may find that you have to do a little bit of both.

These steps will require continuous upkeep, reassessment, and renewal. Use your weekly money meetings to improve your budget. It takes trial and error to get your budget to work for you. After about three months of regular budgeting, money meetings and necessary budget adjustments, your budget should be working well for you. But you are going to have to get your hands dirty and really work your budget during this time to get it to where you need it to be. After that, it will be smooth sailing, and you will have a budget that can work for you for the rest of your life. When you experience occupational or other changes that influence your income and expenses in the future, you will adjust your budget accordingly.

A note about your budget—it really does not matter how much income you receive each month. Whether you are living off of student loans, receive a paycheck from social security, or have irregular income from a non-salaried position, you can create a budget. A budget is less about income and more about your habits of not overspending.

My budget:

INCREASE YOUR INCOME

Everyone has the ability to increase their income. Now is the time where you will look into your finances with more scrutiny. Do you have enough to make ends meet—to cover all of your expenses, make all the necessary payments on your debt, and otherwise meet your financial goals? Most importantly, are you happy with your income? If so, your income is probably ok. If not, or if you want to make more aggressive payments to debt or savings, increase discretionary funds, or create and meet new additional financial goals, you may want to increase your income.

There is no shortage of ways that you can increase the money that you bring into your household. You can do simple tasks like taking surveys online or earning cash back rebates for your grocery shopping. You can start a blog or an online business. You can take a second job in the evenings or on weekends. You can teach English online. You can ask for a raise. If a raise is not feasible, you can apply for another job that pays you better. There is no shortage of ways—but you must choose how you will proceed and then follow through with it. And remember, the only limitations on your income are the limitations that you put on yourself.

Sit down and brainstorm ways that you will increase your income. What will you trade for money? What product could you create? What services could you provide? Write down the first things that come into your mind. Allow yourself to sit and ponder for however long it takes to come up with ideas. Don't label your ideas with any judgment. For example, you might think of a product you could create. That thought might be immediately followed with "No, that's a dumb idea." Drop the judgment. Right now, we are engaging in a judgment-free brainstorming session. Later, you can decide whether to pursue the idea or not.

Now that you have allowed yourself to tap into the creative part of your brain, ideas will start coming to you about how you will increase your income. As they come to you, be sure to write them down either in the space provided above or in another journal.

Your next activity will be to filter out the ideas that you wish to pursue from the ideas that you do not wish to pursue. Come up with a plan on how you will pursue those ideas. What is the first step you will take to pursue your plan? Will you apply for a new job? A second job? Will you create something? How will you create it? Who can you talk to that will be able to help you? Take the first step. After all, a journey of 1,000 miles begins with a single step. You never know where your ideas will take you if you will continue to pursue them. And then persevere after that. And then persevere some more.

Perseverance is a characteristic that almost all successful people have in common. I mention this because in the pursuit of increasing your income, you may have an idea that people around you will think is absurd. They may think that you are crazy for pursuing your idea. You will likely face some form of negativity or pushback to your idea. And if you believe in your idea, if it is one that *you* wish to pursue, you will have to persevere in spite of the people around you who may disagree. And when I say people, I am talking about people that are otherwise your support system. It may take some work convincing your spouse, parents, close friends, and other family members that otherwise are supportive of you. Do not allow any negativity into your mind. If someone is negative about your idea, you must block that out. Recall from Phase II that positivity is *everything* when it comes to financial success.

PHASE III SUMMARY OF TASKS

Weekly meal planning

Weekly money meetings

Phase III workouts

Create a budget

Increase income

PHASE III WORKOUTS

WEEK 5

DAY 1: LEGS

      CARDIO: 20 MINUTES (FASTED)

      STRENGTH:

          LUNGE KICKS 5X20 (PER LEG) FOR SPEED

          SQUATS 5X20 FOR SPEED

          LYING LEG CURL 5X15

          JUMP SQUATS 5X20

          100 CRUNCHES

      CARDIO: 20 MINUTES YOUR CHOICE

DAY 2 CHEST AND TRICEPS

      CARDIO: 20 MINUTES (FASTED)

      STRENGTH:

          CHEST FLYS 4X10

          PUSHUPS 3X10

          STANDING ONE ARM CHEST FLYS 2X12, PER ARM

          TRICEPS PULL DOWN, 3X12

          LYING TRICEPS PULL DOWN 3X12

          TRICEP DIPS 3X12

          100 RUSSIAN TWISTS

      CARDIO: 20 MIN

DAY 3: CARDIO: 40 MINUTES (LIGHT)
DAY 4: BACK AND BICEPS
    CARDIO: 20 MINUTES (FASTED)
    STRENGTH:
        UNDERHAND PULL UPS 4X10
        CHIN UPS 4X10
        BOW POSE 3X12
        STRAIGHT ARM PULL DOWN 7X20
        CONCENTRATION CURLS 4X15 PER ARM
        BICEP CURLS 3X12 PER ARM
        100 RUSSIAN TWISTS
    CARDIO: 20 MINUTES

DAY 5: SHOULDERS ABS AND CALVES

    CARDIO: 20 MINUTES (FASTED)

    STRENGTH:

        SHOULDER PUSHUPS 4X15

        SIDE LATERAL RAISES 5X20

        SHOULDER ROWS 5X20

        WEIGHTED SIT UPS 5X20

        LYING LEG THRUSTS 3X15

        CALF RAISES 5X20

    CARDIO: 20 MINUTES

DAY 6: LEGS

    CARDIO: 20 MINUTES

    STRENGTH:

        SUPERSET:

            JUMPING LUNGES 2X30 (15 PER SIDE) ALTERNATING WITH LYING LEG CURLS 2X20

        SUPERSET:

            3 SETS OF 40 WALKING LUNGES ALTERNATING WITH 3 SETS OF 15-20 LEG CURLS (PER LEG)

            SQUATS 3X50

            3X40 WALKING LUNGES

            3X20 HORSE KICKS

DAY 7: CARDIO: 40 MINUTES (LIGHT)

WEEK 6

DAY 1: HIIT (DO AS MANY REPS AS POSSIBLE IN 1 MIN)

> 1 MINUTE EACH:
>> JUMPING JACKS
>> BODY WEIGHT SQUATS
>> PUSH UPS
>> WALL SIT
>> CRUNCHES
>
> REST 60 SECOND, REPEAT SET 2-3XS
> 1 MINUTE EACH:
>> TUCK JUMPS
>> ALTERNATING LUNGES
>> TRICEP DIPS
>> BURPEES
>> BICYCLE CRUNCHES
>
> REST 60 SECONDS, REPEAT SET 2-3XS
> 1 MINUTE EACH:
>> JABS
>> PLANK
>> HIP THRUSTS
>> MOUNTAIN CLIMBERS
>> FIRE HYDRANT KICKS
>
> REST 60 SECONDS, REPEAT SET 2-3XS

DAY 2: BACK

> 50 PULL UPS
> 50 ROWS
> 50 STRAIGHT ARM PULL DOWNS
>> REPEAT 4XS

DAY 3: CARDIO, 1 HOUR

DAY 4: LEGS AND SHOULDERS

> 50 SQUAT TO SHOULDER PRESS
> 50 WALKING LUNGES (25/SIDE)

50 CALF RAISES

50 SIDE LATERAL RAISES

REPEAT 4XS

DAY 5: CHEST AND TRICEPS

10 BURPEES

10 INCH WORM PUSH UPS

20 TRICEP DIPS

20 TRICEP PUSH UPS

REPEAT 4-5XS, FOR TIME

DAY 6: CORE

100 CRUNCHES

1 MINUTE PLANK

1 MINUTE SIDE PLANK, PER SIDE

100 RUSSIAN TWISTS

REPEAT 5XS

20 MINUTES CARDIO

DAY 7: REST

PHASE IV

SELF CONTROL

Out of the night that covers me,
Black as the Pit from pole to pole,
I thank whatever gods may be
For my unconquerable soul.

In the fell clutch of circumstance,
I have not winced nor cried aloud:
Under the bludgeonings of chance
My head bloody, but unbowed...

It matters not how strait the gate,
How charged with punishments the scroll,
**I am the master of my fate:
I am the captain of my soul.**

–William Ernest Henley "Invictus"

The Purpose of this Program

The purpose of this program is to get you into shape physically and financially. The greatest inhibitor to your success in either of these areas is, undoubtedly, self-control. Anytime we are trying to change or correct behavior, we have to consider the true, underlying problem. When it comes to overspending, overeating, and failing to work out, the root of the problem is often self-control, or, more accurately, the lack of self-control. Thus, in order to succeed in this program, it is prudent to have a basic understanding of self-control—what it is, how it operates, and how you can make it work for you.

What is self-control?

Self-control is one's ability to regulate behavior in the face of temptations or other impulses. Self-control is governed by the brain's prefrontal cortex. Young children have a tough time exerting self-control because the prefrontal cortex is not yet fully developed. Think of your brain like a computer. The prefrontal cortex is like the computer's processor.

Self-control is critical to your success, not only in this program, but in every aspect of your life. In previous Phases, we discussed earning credibility with yourself. Exercising self-control helps you earn credibility with yourself. Being a person that you view as credible will inevitably boost your self-esteem. Having a healthy self-esteem will in turn help you accomplish your goals and ultimately help you exercise even more self-control.

One thing that makes self-control difficult is that there are few people who actually exercise it. There are probably not many good examples in your life. Indeed, we live in an indulgent society. We are inundated with messages that we should indulge ourselves at every turn. In addition, almost anything we want is available at our fingertips with just a few clicks of a button. We can finance products and "pay later" for most anything. We can choose to put tasty, fatty, sugary foods in our bodies which provide instant but fleeting satisfaction. With all of this temptation, how are we supposed to exercise self-control?

You can improve your self-control with sleep, sobriety, and proper nutrition.

While self-control is certainly difficult, the good news is that there are plenty of things that you can do to improve your ability to control yourself, such as getting enough sleep, practicing sobriety, and getting proper nutrition.

Sleep

First, to prime yourself best to exercise self-control, you must get enough sleep. Research shows that the prefrontal cortex (the part of your brain that handles self-control, the computer processer) operates best when you are well rested. What does it mean to be well rested? Most Americans have no idea. Because they aren't.

According to the National Sleep Foundation[xii], adults between the ages of 18-64 require seven to nine hours of sleep in a twenty-four-hour period. In reality, most adults get far less sleep than that. And it certainly influences our ability to control ourselves. Imagine a typical scenario where you did not get enough rest at night. You went to bed late. You were up binge watching a TV show because you felt like you needed to relax after a long and stressful day at work. You also consumed several high-calorie, sugary foods to stay awake watching your show. You eventually turned off the television and tried to go to sleep. Your body was jittery, and your mind was racing. Eventually you fell asleep. Your alarm clock went off early because you have a job. You woke up feeling groggy, and you had a food hangover from the night before. So you skipped breakfast, didn't work out (too tired) and slowly got to your office. At about 10:00 a.m., you drank a caffeinated beverage. You washed it down with a donut.

And then you worked a long, stressful day again. You came home that night, ate greasy, convenient food, and stayed up late again, trying to relax. Then the cycle repeats over and over.

All because you just need sleep! Make a commitment today to start getting to sleep at night. It impacts every facet of your life.

It is not as easy as it sounds for some people. But you can do this for yourself just as you would help a child to get to sleep. Children have bedtimes and bedtime routines. There is a reason for this. It sets cues in their bodies and minds that they should prepare for sleep.

Set the stage for sleep. Give yourself a set bedtime every night. In the hour before your bedtime, set the stage for sleep. You can do this by dimming the lights around your home. Try to avoid vigorous exercise during this hour. (But please note that exercise helps you sleep better through the night, no matter what time of day it occurs. So if it's middle of the night restlessness you face, exercise during the day may be the cure.) Turn off the TV and try to avoid other electronic devices—such light exposure and mental stimulation promotes wakefulness. When your bedtime comes, drop whatever you are doing and go to sleep—every night.

Sobriety

Be more sober. Another primer for excellent self-control is, unsurprisingly, sobriety. Alcohol and drugs harm your brain's ability to make good choices—choices that you would normally choose if you were sober. One research study showed how alcohol dulls the brain signal that warns people they are making a mistake.[xiii] While the drinker is aware of the mistake, alcohol seems to cause them to care less about it. Other research also shows that alcohol damages the part of the brain that governs self-control permanently.[xiv] So make self-control easier on yourself and pass on the alcohol—at least most of the time.

In addition, alcohol is typically packed with calories—usually at least 100 empty calories per serving. This means that for every drink you have, you would need to run at least one mile to negate the caloric intake. And calories are of course much higher in sugary alcoholic drinks.

Nutrition

Eat healthy. Lastly, eating healthy (following your nutrition guide) actually aids in the prefrontal cortex's functioning. In other words, when you eat healthy, your brain functions better. When your brain functions better, it helps you make better choices. This has cyclical benefits—the more you eat healthy, the more your brain will be able to help you make healthier choices in the future.

Relatedly, your brain requires certain levels of glucose for optimal performance. That means if your brain has access to the right amount of glucose, it makes it easier to make good, healthy choices. If your body desperately needs glucose, it will ultimately crave sugar, and we all know that once you start desperately craving something, it is much harder to resist. To that end, this is one of the reasons we will not be engaging in any practices that negatively impact glucose functioning in this program. We will not be starving ourselves, cutting off all carbohydrates, or anything else extreme.

A last word about self-control—think about self-control as if it were a muscle. When we exercise and build muscles, we become stronger and it becomes easier to exercise—when we exercise self-control, it becomes stronger within us and it becomes easier to exercise that muscle.

"That which we persist in doing becomes easier for us to do; not that the nature of the thing itself is changed, but that our power to do is increased." – Ralph Waldo Emerson

Part of the reason that you are spending too much money, eating poorly, and failing to exercise is that you have been not been exercising self-control for a long time. In other words, you are simply in the habit of not exercising self-control. As they say, old habits die hard. But they *can* die, and you can change. The way toward change is by digging to the root of the problem, which we will do by practicing self-control until self-control becomes your new habit. There is a reason that this program is ten weeks long—it gives you enough time to practice and refine new behaviors that you can carry with you for life.

Remember that self-denial is not restrictive. It is liberating. It is the pathway to freedom. It is power.

PARTICIPATE IN A NO SPEND CHALLENGE

To give yourself practice in exercising self-control, you will participate in a "No Spend Challenge" during this Phase.

If you are not familiar with the idea of a no-spend challenge, it is as simple as it sounds. For a period of time, you will not spend money on *anything*. That's right. Not a penny. That period of time will be a full work week. That means from Monday to Friday, you will not spend any money. Perform this challenge on the second week of this Phase (week 8).

This challenge will of course require some mental and

physical preparation. You will need to go to the grocery store and plan meals before the no-spend workweek starts. Be sure that you have enough for breakfasts, lunches, dinners, and snacks each day. You will need to fill up on gas for the week. You will have to be mentally prepared to say no or come up with alternatives if you are invited to social activities that cost money, including meals.

Now, there are exceptional circumstances. For example, you might commute to work several hours each week, making it infeasible to not buy gas during this time. In such a circumstance, allow yourself to spend money on gas, but nothing else. You may only make an exception if it is something that you truly could not have planned ahead for.

PHASE IV SUMMARY OF TASKS

Weekly meal planning

Weekly money meetings

No spend challenge

Phase IV workouts

PHASE IV WORKOUTS

WEEK 7

DAY 1: HIIT (AS MANY REPS AS POSSIBLE IN 1 MIN, RESTING AS NECESSARY)

        1 MINUTE EACH:
- JUMPING JACKS
- BODY WEIGHT SQUATS
- PUSH UPS
- WALL SIT
- CRUNCHES

        REST 60 SECONDS, REPEAT SET 2-3XS

        1 MINUTE EACH:
- TUCK JUMPS
- ALTERNATING LUNGES
- TRICEP DIPS
- BURPEES
- BICYCLE CRUNCHES

        REST 60 SECONDS, REPEAT SET 2-3XS

        1 MINUTE EACH:
- JABS
- PLANK
- HIP THRUSTS
- MOUNTAIN CLIMBERS
- FIRE HYDRANT KICKS

        REST 60 SECONDS, REPEAT SET 2-3XS

DAY 2: BACK
- 50 PULL UPS (ASSISTED AS NEEDED)
- 50 WEIGHT ROWS
- 50 STRAIGHT ARM PULL DOWNS
- REPEAT 4XS

DAY 3: CARDIO: 1 HOUR

DAY 4: LEGS + SHOULDERS

      50 SQUAT TO SHOULDER PRESS

      50 WALKING LUNGES (25/SIDE)

      50 CALF RAISES

      50 SIDE LATERAL RAISES

      REPEAT 4XS

DAY 5: CHEST AND TRICEPS

      10 BURPEES

      10 INCH WORM PUSH UPS

      20 TRICEP DIPS

      20 TRICEP PUSH UPS

      REPEAT 4-5XS, FOR TIME

DAY 6: CORE

      100 CRUNCHES

      1 MINUTE PLANK

      1 MINUTE SIDE PLANK, PER SIDE

      100 RUSSIAN TWISTS

      REPEAT 5XS

      CARDIO: 20 MINUTES

DAY 7: REST

WEEK 8

DAY 1: CHEST AND TRICEPS

      CARDIO: 20 MINUTES (FASTED)

      STRENGTH:

            CHEST FLYS 5X10

            PUSH UPS 2X MAX REPS

            STANDING ONE ARM FLYS 2X10 PER ARM

            TRICEPS PULL DOWN 3X10

            LYING TRICEPS EXTENSIONS 3X10

            STANDING TRICEPS EXTENSION 3X10

            100 RUSSIAN TWISTS

      CARDIO: 20 MIN

DAY 2: CARDIO: 40 MINUTES

DAY 3: LEGS

    CARDIO: 20 MINUTES (FASTED)

    STRENGTH:

        LUNGE KICKS 5X15 PER LEG

        SQUATS 5X20 FOR SPEED

        LYING LEG CURL 5X15

        JUMP SQUATS 5X20

        100 CRUNCHES

    CARDIO: 20 MINUTES

DAY 4: CARDIO: 40 MINUTES (LIGHT)

DAY 5: BACK AND BICEPS

    CARDIO: 20 MINUTES (FASTED)

    STRENGTH:

        UNDERHAND PULL UPS 4X10

        ROWS 4X12

        LOCUST POSE 3X12 PULSE

        STRAIGHT ARM PULL DOWN 7X15

        CONCENTRATION CURLS 4X15 (PER ARM)

        BICEP CURLS 3X15 (PER ARM)

        100 RUSSIAN TWISTS

    CARDIO: 20 MINUTES

DAY 6: SHOULDERS ABS AND CALVES

    CARDIO: 20 MINUTES (FASTED)

    STRENGTH:

        SHOULDER PUSH UPS 4X20

        SIDE LATERAL RAISES 4X20

        UPRIGHT ROWS 3X15

        REAR DELT RAISE 7X15

        CRUNCHES 3X20

        CALF RAISES, 6X20

    CARDIO: 20 MINUTES

DAY 7: LEGS

CARDIO: 20 MINUTES

STRENGTH:

SUPERSET:

JUMPING LUNGES 2X30 (15 PER SIDE) ALTERNATING WITH LYING LEG CURLS 2X20

SUPERSET:

WALKING LUNGES 3X40 ALTERNATING WITH LYING LEG CURLS 3X15

SQUATS 3X50

WALKING LUNGES 1X40

HORSE KICKS 1X20

PHASE V

EVALUATE

"Ignorance, the root and stem of all evil."

- Plato

The first time I went snowboarding, I was with my older brother. He is the type of person that is naturally good at everything he does the first time he tries it. He was breezing down the mountain like he had been doing it for years. I, on the other hand, was having a difficult time navigating my board.

We started out on a path that had a steep cliff on one side and a lot of trees on the other side. I was trying with all my might to just make my merry way down the mountain. I did not want to fall off the edge of a cliff. I did not want to get stuck in the trees. I was doing everything I could to not go towards the cliff or the trees—it was all I could think about. Consequently, as I would gain speed, I kept ending up on the edge of the cliff or in the trees.

On one such occurrence, my brother stopped me and said

something that has stuck with me. "Stop focusing on where you don't want to go. Start looking where you want to go. You will always go in the direction that you are looking."

As I was snowboarding, all I was thinking about was where I did not want to go. And that is precisely *why* I ended up there—because it was all I could think about. It was in the forefront of my mind, blocking out any focus on how to get to where I wanted to go. Instead, I should have been thinking about where I *did* want to go and focusing in that direction. My then nineteen-year-old brother probably had no idea how profound his words were and how deeply they would impact decisions I would make later in life.

Learning to navigate your financial and physical fitness is, in a sense, like snowboarding. You have to focus on where you want to go in order to get there. If you focus on the wrong things, you will go the wrong way. The final phase of this program is the **evaluation** phase. You must ensure that you are looking in the right direction to get where you want to go with your physical and financial fitness.

In Phase I, you set goals and made plans. Where are you now? Are you still headed in the right direction? Are you continuing to focus in on your goals? Or are you paralyzed by fear? Have you experienced some setbacks?

Staying focused on your goals takes constant vigilance. If you look away from where you want to go, even for a moment, you will get off course. Even the smallest degree of change in direction can lead you somewhere you do not want to be. Staying focused on your goals will not always be easy, which is why you must constantly evaluate where you are and where you are headed. If you are experiencing a lot of adversity in working towards your goals, you will know that you are on the right track. The universe tends to hedge up the way in the moments just before great things happen. Henry Ford said, "When everything seems to be going against you, remember that the airplane takes off against the wind, not with it." If you are experiencing adversity, just hold on tight. Stay the course. In just a few moments, things are going to take off for you, and you just might end up exactly where you want to be.

After completing Phases I-IV, where are your finances? Where is your physical fitness? Is it all where you want it to be? Make the changes you need to today to get where you want to go. Has your weight plateaued? Cut more or burn more calories. Did you overspend last weekend? Forgive yourself, resolve not to do it again, and trudge on. You do not have to execute all of your plans perfectly. But what will make the difference in whether you succeed or not is the extent to which you learn from your failures, evaluate why you failed, and try again.

Remember Lot's Wife.

There is an illustrious story from the Bible in Genesis 19 about an important woman. Despite the importance of what her story symbolizes, we don't even know her name, only that she was "Lot's wife."

God commanded Lot and his family to leave the wicked city of Sodom and told them, in no uncertain terms, that he was going to destroy the city and that they could not look back. We don't know much about Lot. But, for purposes of this discussion, let's entertain some ideas. Perhaps Lot was wealthy. Perhaps Lot had family heirlooms that were meaningful to him. Maybe he had just finished building his dream home on the perfect lot—pun intended. Would it be easy for you to leave home in those circumstances? Well, it apparently wasn't for Lot's wife. As she left the city of Sodom with her family, she affectionately looked back, and for doing so, was transformed into a pillar of salt.

What was so wrong with her looking to the past?

Simply this— she should not have been looking to the past *longingly*. Perhaps the real problem with Lot's wife was that she wanted to go back to the way things were, despite having received divine guidance that she and her family were meant for something greater.

On your journey to physical and financial success, you might find yourself like Lot's wife—longing to go back to the way things were. It seems easier to eat convenient fast food. It is easier to *not* work out. It is easy to pretend not to care about your money and live in the moment—buying whatever you want, eating whatever you want, doing whatever you want. But remember Lot's wife. Remember where that longing for the past will get you. For Lot's wife—it got her turned into a pillar of salt. You don't need that extra sodium in your life anyway. Keep your focus on your goals.

A final note about Lot's wife—do not make the mistake of completely forgetting about the past. The past is to be learned from. We must evaluate ourselves and where we have been in order to improve. We must use the mistakes we have made, the financial and fitness slip-ups, to help fortify us. When we can better identify our weaknesses, it is much easier to prepare for and overcome them.

In this final phase, you will help keep yourself focused on your goals by creating reminder notes, evaluating your physical fitness, and evaluating your budget, spending, and income. The first task is to create reminder notes.

CREATE REMINDER NOTES

Create reminders around your house, office, or anywhere you spend significant time, to remind you to stay on track. Every year, my husband and I come up with a theme that we want to work on throughout the year. One year, we chose "happy and healthy," and we simply wrote the phrase on a post-it note and stuck it in our car, bathroom, on our fridge and in our wallets. As we got ready in the morning, drove to work or school, and shopped, we were reminded of our goals. It helped our actions stay consistent with our goals. You could simply write the word "Phased" and place it around your home to remind you to stay the course and keep to your goals. Whatever you write, make it short and sweet, and let it serve as a reminder to you about what you now stand for.

EVALUATE YOUR PHYSICAL FITNESS

There are two weeks left in this program. Is your physical fitness better than it was when you started? Have you achieved any of your physical fitness goals yet? What can you do to improve? Sit down and consider things that you can do to improve your physical fitness. If you have not achieved your goals yet, why not? Has enough time passed to allow you to achieve them? What could you do to improve? What things are setting you back?

If you have achieved all or some of your goals, what will you do next? How can you improve? What will you do to maintain your fitness? You may write in the space below or in your own journal or notes if you wish. But do be sure to write down how you will improve. Recall from Phase I that writing your aspirations down makes all the difference.

EVALUATE YOUR BUDGET, INCOME, AND EXPENSES

Recall from Phase III that creating the perfect budget takes time and effort. Is your current budget working for you? Are you finding that you have too many expenses to make your budget work for you? How can you improve your budget? Where can you cut expenses? How can you increase your income even more? What is working in your budget? What is not? If you share money with someone else, discuss this with them at your next money meeting.

PHASE V SUMMARY OF TASKS:

Weekly meal planning

Weekly money meetings

Create reminder notes

Evaluate your physical fitness

Evaluate your budget, income, and expenses

Phase V workouts

PHASE V WORKOUTS

WEEK 9

DAY 1: ABS, CHEST, AND TRICEPS
INCLINE PUSHUPS 3X12, 1 MINUTE RUN IN PLACE BETWEEN SETS
DECLINE PUSHUPS 3X12, 1 MINUTE MOUNTAIN CLIMBERS BETWEEN SETS
PUSHUPS 3X12, 1 MINUTE JUMPING JACKS BETWEEN SETS
TRICEP DIPS 4X15, 1 MINUTE JUMPING SQUATS BETWEEN SETS
CRUNCHES 4X20
PLATINUM PLANKS
    HOLD FOR 45 SECONDS THEN DIRECTLY INTO SIDE PLANK 45 SECONDS PER SIDE
CARDIO: 20 MINUTES

DAY 2: LEGS AND SHOULDERS
SHOULDER PRESS 4X12, 1 MINUTE HIGH KNEES BETWEEN SETS
ALTERNATING SHOULDER PRESS 3X12, 1 MINUTE BUTT KICKS BETWEEN SETS
UPRIGHT ROWS 3X12, 1 MINUTE SPRINT
JUMP SQUATS 4X15, 1 MIUTE JUMPING LUNGES, ALTERNATING LEGS
DEADLIGHTS 4X12, 1 MINUTE MOUNTAIN CLIMBERS
WALKING LUNGES 4X20 PER LEG, 1 MINUTE OF FRONT KICKS
CALF RAISES 6X20 REPS

DAY 3: BACK AND BICEPS

    CARDIO: 20 MINUTES (FASTED)

    STANDING ROWS 4X12, 1 MINUTE BUTT KICKS BETWEEN SETS

    WIDE GRIP PULL UPS (PULL UP BAR OR BANDS) 4X12 MODIFIED AS NEEDED, 1 MINUTE HIGH KNEES BETWEEN SETS

    UNDERARM PULL UPS (PULL UP BAR OR BANDS) 4X12 MODIFIED AS NEEDED, 1 MINUTE LATERAL HOPS BETWEEN SETS

    BICEP CURLS 4X12, 1 MINUTE MOUNTAIN CLIMBERS BETWEEN SETS

    SUPERMAN POSE 4X15, 1 MINUTE BOX JUMPS (OR KNEE TUCKS) BETWEEN SETS

DAY 4: CARDIO: 30 MINUTES

DAY 5: ABS, CHEST, AND TRICEPS

    INCLINE PUSHUPS 3X12, 1 MINUTE RUN IN PLACE BETWEEN SETS

    DECLINE PUSHUPS 3X12, 1 MINUTE MOUNTAIN CLIMBERS BETWEEN SETS

    PUSHUPS 3X12, 1 MINUTE JUMPING JACKS BETWEEN SETS

    TRICEP DIPS 4X15, 1 MINUTE JUMPING SQUATS BETWEEN SETS

    CRUNCHES 4X20

    PLATINUM PLANKS

        HOLD FOR 45 SECONDS THEN DIRECTLY INTO SIDE PLANK 45 SECONDS PER SIDE

    CARDIO: 20 MINUTES

DAY 6: LEGS AND SHOULDERS

SHOULDER PRESS 4X12, 1 MINUTE HIGH KNEES BETWEEN SETS

ALTERNATING SHOULDER PRESS 3X12, 1 MINUTE BUTT KICKS BETWEEN SETS

UPRIGHT ROWS 3X12, 1 MINUTE SPRINT

JUMP SQUATS 4X15, 1 MIUTE JUMPING LUNGES, ALTERNATING LEGS

DEADLIGHTS 4X12, 1 MINUTE MOUNTAIN CLIMBERS

WALKING LUNGES 4X20 PER LEG, 1 MINUTE OF FRONT KICKS

CALF RAISES 6X20 REPS

DAY 7: REST

WEEK 10

DAY 1: LEGS

    CARDIO: 20 MINUTES (FASTED)

    STRENGTH:

        LUNGE KICKS 5X20 (PER LEG) FOR SPEED

        SQUATS 5X20 FOR SPEED

        LYING LEG CURL 5X15

        JUMP SQUATS 5X20

        100 CRUNCHES

    CARDIO: 20 MINUTES

DAY 2: CHEST AND TRICEPS

    CARDIO: 20 MINUTES (FASTED)

    STRENGTH:

        CHEST FLYS 4X10

        PUSH UPS 3X10

        STANDING ONE ARM FLYS 2X12, PER ARM

        TRICEPS PULL DOWN 3X12

        LYING TRICEPS PULL DOWN 3X12

        TRICEP DIPS 3X12

        100 RUSSIAN TWISTS

    CARDIO: 20 MIN

DAY 3: CARDIO: 40 MINUTES (LIGHT)

DAY 4: BACK AND BICEPS

    CARDIO: 20 MINUTES (FASTED)

    STRENGTH:

        UNDERHAND PULL UPS 4X10

        CHIN UPS 4X10

        BOW POSE 3X12

        STRAIGHT ARM PULL DOWN 7X20

        CONCENTRATION CURLS 4X15 PER ARM

        BICEP CURLS 3X12 PER ARM

        100 RUSSIAN TWISTS

    CARDIO: 20 MINUTES

DAY 5: SHOULDERS ABS AND CALVES

      CARDIO: 20 MINUTES (FASTED)

      STRENGTH:

            SHOULDER PUSH UPS 4X20

            SIDE LATERAL RAISES 4X20

            UPRIGHT ROWS 3X15

            REAR DELT RAISE 7X15

            CRUNCHES 3X20

            CALF RAISES, 6X20

DAY 6: LEGS

      CARDIO: 20 MINUTES

      STRENGTH:

      SUPERSET:

            2X30 JUMPING LUNGES (15 PER SIDE) ALTERNATING WITH

            2X20 LYING LEG CURLS

      SUPERSET:

            3 SETS OF 40 WALKING LUNGES ALTERNATING WITH

            3 SETS OF 15-20 LEG CURLS (PER LEG)

            SQUATS 3X50

            3X40 WALKING LUNGES

            3X20 HORSE KICKS

DAY 7: REST

Congratulations on completing this program. Take time to celebrate all of your progress. If I were there with you, I would throw some confetti and give you a big high-five. But remember that your physical and financial fitness are just like a muscle. You have to put in work to make them strong. If you slack off, they will become weaker. Old habits will try to creep into your life—keep fighting against them. As you achieve goals, set new ones. If you fail at something, pick yourself up and try again. Or, try something new. Never give up. Be proud of yourself for how far you have come in the last ten weeks. The future ahead is bright. Keep up the great work.

[i] Kathryn Vasel, "6 in 10 Americans Don't Have $500 in Savings," *CNN Money*, January 12, 2017, http://money.cnn.com/2017/01/12/pf/americans-lack-of-savings/index.html 2017.

[ii] "Overweight & Obesity Statistics," National Institute of Diabetes and Digestive and Kidney Diseases, last modified August 2017, https://www.niddk.nih.gov/health-information/health-statistics/overweight-obesity.

[iii] Betsy Demitropoulos, "Exercising and Work Performance," *The TJB American Business Magazine*, June 7, 2011, http://www.americanbusinessmag.com/2011/06/exercising-and-work-performance.

[iv]Valerie DeBenedette, "Time Spent Preparing Meals at Home Linked to Healthier Diet," *American Journal of Preventive Medicine,* October 20, 20144. http://www.ajpmonline.org/pb/assets/raw/Health%20Advance/journals/amepre/Time_Spent_Preparing_Meals_at_Home_Linked_to_Healthier_Diet.pdf

[v] *Monsivais, Pablo et al.,* "Time Spent on Home Food Preparation and Indicators of Healthy Eating,*" American Journal of Preventive Medicine,*47, *no.* 6 (December 2014):796-802. http://dx.doi.org/10.1016/j.amepre.2014.07.033

[vi] Brian Tracy, *No Excuses!: The Power of Self-Discipline* (New York: Vanguard Press, reprint 2010).

[vii] Nicholas Boothman, *How to Make People Like You in 90 Seconds or Less* (New York: Workman Publishing Company, reprint 2008).

[viii] "Long-term Investment Performance," Raymond James & Associates, Inc., Morningstar, last modified March 1, 2011, https://www.raymondjames.com/melvillewealthmanagement/pdfs/long_term_investment_performance.pdf.

[ix] Darren Poke, "Two Travelers, A Story About Optimism," Inspirational stories, last modified July 30, 2010, https://betterlifecoachingblog.com/2010/07/30/the-two-travellers-a-story-about-optimism.

[x] Napoleon Hill, *Think and Grow Rich* (The Ralston Society, 1937).

[xi] Sydney J. Harries, "Do You Act—Or React?" *Chicago Daily News,* 1976. (adapted)

[xii] "National Sleep Foundation Recommends New Sleep Times," National Sleep Foundation, last modified February 2, 2015, https://sleepfoundation.org/press-release/national-sleep-foundation-recommends-new-sleep-times.

[xiii] Bartholow BD, et al., "Alcohol Effects on Performance Monitoring and Adjustment: Affect Modulation and Impairment of Evaluative Cognitive Control," *Journal of Abnormal Psychology,* 121, no.1 (February 2012):173-86, https://doi.org/10.1037/a0023664.

[xiv] Madlen Davies, "Why heavy drinkers can't give up alcohol," *DailyMail.com,* November 18, 2014, http://www.dailymail.co.uk/health/article-2839661/Booze-damages-brain-deals-self-control.html.

www.ingramcontent.com/pod-product-compliance
Lightning Source LLC
Chambersburg PA
CBHW071523220526
45472CB00003B/1122